THE ART OF LUNGEING

PLATE 1

The author with her six-year-old thoroughbred Cranwell, bred by H.M. The Queen. Cranwell was used for all the photographs in this book.

THE ART OF LUNGEING

SYLVIA STANIER

J. A. ALLEN

LONDON & NEW YORK

Stanier, Sylvia
  The art of lungeing
  1. Horse-training
  I. Title
  636.1'08'3   SF 287   77-30236

ISBN 085 131 292 6

Published in 1976 by J. A. Allen & Company Limited,
Reprinted 1977, 1979 and 1982
1, Lower Grosvenor Place,
Buckingham Palace Road,
London, SW1W 0EL.

Book production by Bill Ireson.

Printed and bound in Great Britain by The Devonshire Press,
Torquay, Devon.

CONTENTS

ILLUSTRATIONS

PLATES

(All photographs by D. & J. Studios)

FIGURES

INTRODUCTION

In order to obtain a successful result in any form of training
or schooling, a horse must primarily understand what we want
of him; and secondly, he must not be asked to undertake feats
which he is unable to perform physically. All too often one
sees horses resisting the efforts of their riders or trainers
because of a lack of understanding of these problems. By this,
I do not mean that the horse should get away with everything
and become unruly, but rather that he be carefully trained to
accept all our demands.

Through work on the ground, a great deal can be achieved,
and the foundations of a real rapport between horse and man
can be laid. Lungeing is perhaps one of the best ways of doing
this. It is a lot easier to do than long reining, in fact it is
something everybody can make themselves reasonably
proficient at.

There are three main uses of lungeing:—
(a) To exercise a horse
(b) To school a horse
(c) To jump a horse
I will discuss these in detail in the chapters ahead.

*By skill is the woodcutter superior rather
than by strength.
By skill doth the steersman guide his swift
ship all buffetted by the winds; by skill likewise
doth charioteer get the better of charioteer.*

HOMER'S *Iliad*

I

TACK AND HOW TO FIT IT

There are numerous items of tack required for lungeing and it is important that they fit correctly.

In the simplest form of lungeing, the following things will be needed:—

(1) *Cavasson Headcollar*

This should have a well padded noseband, with a metal surround and three metal rings. The cavasson should be strongly made and the noseband fitted snugly round the horse's head, about four fingers above his nostrils, otherwise it will interfere with the horse's breathing. The noseband must be tight enough to ensure that it does not pull or move round because, if it does, the major source of control over a fresh horse will be lost. It is important to see that the straps on the outside of the horse's face do not get into his eye. I find that if the throat lash straps are put under and round the headstall straps and then fastened in the ordinary way, that this helps to keep the main headstall strap back and therefore away from the eyes.

There are several makes of cavasson headcollars. Some are bigger and heavier than others. The lightest of these is the Wels type, as used in Vienna. Personally I find a simple and not too heavy model is quite satisfactory, and have a preference for the type which fit above the bit.

(2) *Lungeing Rein*

This should be about 6 metres (20 ft) in length (not less, nothing is worse than too short a rein), and made of a strong lightweight material. Most lungeing reins are made of canvas, but personally I prefer the nylon variety as it is lighter, yet

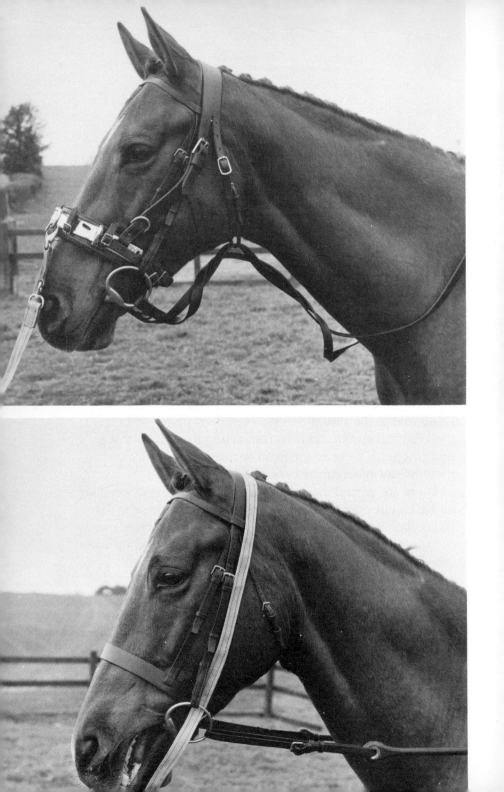

PLATE 2 *(opposite, top)*

The cavasson headcollar and bridle fitted ready for lungeing.

PLATE 3 *(opposite, bottom)*

The lungeing rein attached to the bit, ready to lunge from the bit — near side.

PLATE 4 *(above)*

The same attachment, seen from the off side.

exceedingly strong. There should be a loop at one end, (but do not allow this to go round your wrist, as that would be dangerous) which you can hold in your hand, the spare end of the rein being made into loops of about a foot or so in length. There should be a buckle at the other end to attach to the middle ring of the cavasson, the other two rings are normally used for long rein work. The buckle may be a leather strap and buckle, but, again, I have my own preference and that is for the spring clip metal buckle on a swivel. This is easy to attach, and because of the swivel, prevents any twisting up of the lungeing rein.

(3) *The Whip*
Essential for guiding the horse. It has a long handle and a long lash. The fibre glass variety are probably the most practical, being light and durable. A good tip is to bind the place where the handle and lash divide, with a piece of Elastoplast or tape, so as to prevent the lash from breaking off. Always be careful not to frighten the horse with the whip, use it gently and only when you need to. Carry the whip in the opposite hand to that holding the lungeing rein. On the left rein carry it in the right hand, and unless you want to use it, keep the lash in your hand alongside the handle, and point the whip away behind you, only releasing the lash for use. The horse then realises it is only used when something is required of him. It is a good idea for a beginner to practice a few times, carrying and using the whip without the horse. This way the beginner can learn how to carry the whip without fumbling. The whip should be worked from your wrist.

(4) *Boots*
Certainly if the horse is shod, or even if he is not, it is a good idea to protect his legs whilst lungeing him, with either brushing boots or bandages. The boots should be of the kind

that have four leather buckles for the hind legs, and three for the front legs, with the buckles fastening on the outside. Bandages should, in my opinion, have some cotton wool underneath them to prevent them rubbing or cutting into the tendons and should be either the stretch or cotton type — never the woolly stable ones. There are, of course, many types of protective boots, such as polo boots, foam rubber, and so on. The main thing is to see that the horse's fetlocks and tendons are protected.

The tack so far described is all that is necessary for simple lungeing. However, for certain schooling exercises a bridle and side reins will be needed.

(5) *Bridle*

A simple, jointed, snaffle, preferably with a thick mouthpiece. Make sure the bit is neither too wide nor too narrow. The former rubs and the latter pinches, and comfort is essential. Some people may like to use a Viennese or Fulmer type snaffle. If you do, be careful to see that the side checks are fitted into the small loops on the headpiece of the bridle, otherwise the bit will not be positioned correctly in the horse's mouth. A horse can be lunged in a double bridle, a pelham, or a breaking bit, but I would not advise attaching the side reins to such bits. All nosebands, other than the cavasson, should be loosely adjusted and all comfortable.

One word about fitting the cavasson, if you are lungeing with a bridle on the horse. I prefer to fit the noseband of the cavasson under the side straps of the bridle headpiece, other-wise the bridle will pinch the horse. Unless it is a special Wels cavasson, one should fit the noseband above the bit. (The Wels type fits below the bit.) In any case be sure to look and see that the cavasson and bit do not together cause the horse's lips to get pinched between them; that is, the cavasson must be high enough when above the bit.

(6) *Side reins*

They should be made of fairly narrow leather with a strap and buckle fastening, which is usually attached to the girth, or roller, and the other end of the rein should have a clip for attaching to the ring of the bit. There are two types of side reins, one with strong rubber inserted at about midway, the other made of plain leather throughout. My own preference is for the rubber type of rein, as I feel less damage will be caused to a horse's mouth this way. However, some experts believe that horses learn to lean on the rubber type, and that the more severe all leather rein makes the horse more respectful of the bit and the rein. Side reins are, or should really only be, used in more advanced training, and then the trainer should have attained some proficiency.

The correct fitting of the side rein will be discussed in Chapters V and XI.

Attaching the Lungeing Rein

It is usually best to attach the rein onto the centre ring of the cavasson, and to work the horse from there. However, it is permissable in certain circumstances to attach the rein to the bit. This is done by placing the rein through the bit ring on the near (left) side and taking it over the horse's head and clipping it onto the bit ring on the off (right) side — if one is lungeing on the right rein the procedure is reversed. (*See plates 3 and 4.*) This method is much used on the Continent by certain trainers, but I would suggest that it is, like the side reins, better left to those who are familiar with the techniques of training. Far less damage will be done to the horse's mouth, by people with less experience if they keep the rein on the ring of the cavasson. There is no reason, however, for a keen pupil not to learn to become proficient enough to use the Continental method.

II

FIRST LESSONS

Once a young horse has been led, and handled nicely, the
next step is to teach him to lunge.

There are certain rules which will help us to teach him, or
in fact to teach older horses how to go round correctly.

First of all, having fitted the tack correctly, lead your
horse to a place where there is some form of fence or surround
to the area. If you have a manège or indoor school, so much
the better, but the corner of a field, with perhaps a long pole
laid on two oil drums to cover the open side will suffice.

The important thing is not to take your fresh or unschooled
horse into the middle of a large open field and expect him to
go round you without trouble. The walls or fence of your
arena not only act as extra aids, they also serve as a control,
and enable you to make the horse attentive. Horses are very
long sighted and observant and if they can see things away in
the distance they are apt to look at them, instead of paying
attention to their work.

When you have arrived in the lungeing area, you want to
encourage the horse to walk round you on the left rein. This
is best done by letting out the rein a little and placing yourself more or less in line with the horse's inside (left) hip. Now
you are in a position to "push" him on from behind, and
perhaps touch him gently on the hocks with the whip. If you
want to slow him up, shorten the rein and place yourself
nearer to his shoulder. Sometimes it is a good idea to have a
helper who can walk nearer the horse carrying the whip and
keeping the horse out on the circle, but the helper must work
quietly and know what they are doing, and not hustle the
horse.

At first the horse will be on a rather small circle, 1·5 to 2 metres (5 to 7 ft), which should be gradually increased until the horse is 3 to 4·5 metres (10 to 15 ft) away from you, sometimes even more. The size of circles is an important one when schooling a horse, as in too small a circle the horse can damage himself in several ways. This will be discussed in Chapter IV. Suffice to say then, that in the first lessons the horse learns to go quietly round on the circle and learns to obey the trainer's voice and body position.

I like to give my voice commands — "walk on"; "trot"; "halt" — in the first lessons at a particular place, and that place is one where I know I have control of the horse and can achieve my aim. The association of ideas is important in schooling. For instance, if I have a horse who does not understand halting, I may stop him on the short side of the school facing the next wall — that is on the corner. He has to stop, which is the priority. I will use the same place several times. By making much of him, and using the word "halt", the horse will very soon learn to stop on the word "halt" and it can be used eventually in any part of the arena; and should be.

Having taught the horse to "walk on" and "trot" on the left rein, this process must then be taught on the right rein. This is often quite a lot more difficult. There are, I think, several reasons for this. One being that people apparently always approach horses, including foals, on the left side, so habit comes into it. Then there is the question of the natural curvature of the spine, which seems to make it easier for the horse to proceed to the left. However, it is most important to teach him to go on both reins. If the horse is very disinclined to go to the right, and you have a helper available, it is quite a good idea to have the horse led around you on the circle a few times. The helper should be on the outside of the circle and should gradually fade away once the horse is going. Otherwise, I think the outside wall is the best help, taking the horse in the corner and positioning him on a small circle, always keeping somewhat behind him and walking with him so that he gets the idea of forward movement. Always be careful not to use the whip roughly, carry it behind you and only apply it gently around the hocks, or occasionally towards the ribs, to keep the horse out on the circle.

There are two schools of thought on where the trainer should stand when lungeing. I am quite certain that in the very first lessons he must be prepared to move so as to be able to position and control the horse. Once the horse has learned to obey the trainer, and answers the voice, then the trainer should move as little as possible. Some people like to fix one heel into the ground so as to make certain it is the horse that goes round and not them. Moving around too much is a bad thing, but one must be able to move to apply the whip or to encourage a sluggish horse, or slow one that is going too fast. So I like to move round on a very small circle myself. The lungeing rein itself should be reasonably taut — not slack. The rein hand should be carried at about hip level — not high in the air. Working on the left rein, the lungeing rein should be held in the left hand, and the whip in the right hand, and vice versa.

A horse should be taught eventually to halt (from the walk) on the circle and to stand still. He should stand calmly and only come into you when you take a step towards, or call, him. It is a very tiresome habit if a horse learns to turn in whenever he feels like it. So being taught to halt is a discipline, and teaches the horse to start to obey.

Always make much of the horse when he has done something correctly. He will learn very quickly to understand. Proceed slowly, this is the keystone to success.

The canter is a pace which should not be introduced really until the horse is thoroughly conversant with the walk and the trot. Also, cantering a young unbalanced horse on a small

PLATE 5 *(opposite, top)*

The horse being lunged off the cavasson. This photograph shows the horse at the commencement of the lesson, with head up and stiff back.

PLATE 6 *(above)*

The horse beginning to lengthen and lower his neck.

PLATE 7 *(opposite, bottom)*

The horse has now relaxed, and is moving his back nicely and appears softer and more supple throughout.

circle is not a good thing. Later on the canter can be very useful to work certain back muscles. Just as the horse must learn to stand still calmly, so he must also learn to start off quietly. Nothing is worse, or even more dangerous, than a horse which dashes off as you start to lunge him, giving a good kick as he does so.

Through the lungeing rein, the horse should be taught calm obedience, achieved on the trainer's part with patience and understanding.

The length of your first lessons depends on circumstances, but assuming that the horse is either being turned out for a few hours, or even in the case of an older horse being ridden, about 10 minutes on either rein to start with, building up to 20 minutes on each rein is advisable. The work should be slow and easy. Really in the very beginning, much of the work comes into the category of handling the horse as opposed to working the horse.

III

EXERCISING

To exercise a fit hunter, by lungeing it for instance, can be very useful if the horse has a sore back, or if its rider is away. But it would not be a good thing to do every day, without some riding. Riding horses need riding. However, to get the freshness off him, or to keep him going for a day when riding is impossible, 30 minutes or so on the lunge is most useful.

Lungeing is a method used to exercise thoroughbred stallions which are not being ridden, but must be kept well muscled up. They are often worked for an hour or more. I would suggest putting such a horse — when we know he is fit, and when we know he is familiar with being lunged — on a big circle to the left, some 20 metres (65 ft 8 ins) in diameter and allow him to trot on at a fairly active trot. Keep him going in trot for up to 10 minutes at a time, then allow him to walk and then, if the horse is conversant with it, do the same on the right rein, finishing up by letting him walk quietly to cool off.

Naturally one must watch the horse and see by his behaviour if he needs more, or less, work. If he sweats and blows a lot, then the trotting work will have to be less than 10 minutes at a time and include more walking. On the other hand a big, strong, fresh horse may well trot round happily for up to 20 minutes. It is important that a fresh horse be kept going forwards and the question of the handler standing still while the horse defies you may need to be modified.

Some horses may like to do some cantering, and provided they do not buck and kick too much this may be a good idea. But watch that the horse does not kick himself or trip up and fall, or for that matter go into a disunited and very unbalanced canter which may well damage him. Careering round on the

PLATE 8

Ready to lunge (working from the bit), side reins attached, and wearing protective boots on the fore legs.

lungeing rein is not a good idea. As in everything else, the horse should go calmly. The horse should certainly have boots on, or bandages on all his legs, and the ground on which he works should be neither rough and stony, nor too deep. Nor should the horse be exercised in a place where he can get away from his handler.

IV

SCHOOLING HORSES YOUNG AND OLD

The true schooling of the horse on the lungeing rein should not differ in its objects from that of mounted schooling.

Having taught the young horse obedience and calmness, one can then start to look at his paces and at his outline. The paces should be active, the rhythm regular and the steps even. From the ground the trainer has the advantage of being able to see if this is so. From the horse's point of view he can achieve this more easily, without the weight of a rider to unbalance him, and his muscles, tendons and joints can strengthen up well before he is eventually mounted. Lungeing for a time each day, is a very useful part of a horse's training.

In the young horse, one looks for a working trot, with the horse's hind feet tracking well up to the imprint of the front ones, and the horse's neck stretching out and downwards. To achieve the tracking up, the horse must be moving forwards actively, this should enable him to use his back correctly, which is a criterion of good schooling. The neck being stretched out and down, will enable the horse to use the top (crest) muscle on his neck, whilst the strong muscle underneath his neck will not be used so much and should thus, gradually reduce itself. Thus, the horse should come into a good rounded outline. Later, when the horse starts more collected work, he will be correctly muscled to achieve it. To obtain a nice working trot, one must encourage the horse forwards on a circle of about 15 metres (49 ft 3 ins) diameter. The lungeing rein should have a nice contact with the hand, which may have to "play" the rein by tightening and relaxing the contact, to ask the horse to stretch down. With the young horse I prefer to see him worked without the side reins, and to achieve a nice loose and supple neck at this stage. I do not like to see a horse in a constricted position. He must learn to balance himself by using his neck and bring his hocks under him, particularly if he is going to be an eventer or jumper. It is at a later stage, that the side reins should be introduced — when the horse has learned to go in his own balance, is using his back and neck, and is ready for the next stage of training, when he is asked to carry himself in a more advanced outline.

The size of the circles can be varied, but remember that the horse's hind feet must follow in the track of his fore feet, but his quarters should not swing out of line of the circle, which they will do if the circle is too small.

The paces should, as well as being active, show that the horse is working both his hindquarters and his forehand equally well — which he should do if he is also using his back and his neck. The horse can be encouraged occasionally to show some lengthened steps in his trot, but not so much as to cause him to lose his balance, that is to canter, or to become very uneven.

Another very useful exercise on the lunge is to halt the horse and to go and stand close to his head, having shortened up the rein. Put the left hand on the cavasson to hold it. Then, by holding the whip in the right hand, touch the horse behind the elbow (in the region of where a girth would fit), with the handle of the whip making him take a step with his **left hind leg sideways.** In other words to take one, or perhaps two, steps of a turn on the forehand, thus learning to "move away from the leg." This is a useful exercise for use when mounted, and also a preliminary lesson in lateral suppleness. Only do one, or possibly two, steps at a time. Try and not let the horse step or run back. The inside hind leg must always pass in front of the other hind leg — never behind it. Do the exercise on both sides, and make much of the horse when he completes it.

The trot is always said to be the pace at which one works a

horse, and the walk the pace at which one introduces things and rewards the horse. The canter is usually for the horse a rather exciting pace, it is quicker and his whole body weight is propelled with some force. So it stands to reason, that the canter is introduced for purely schooling purposes at a later stage than are the other two paces. However, it should be introduced sooner or later, if only to teach the horse to lead with the inside, or correct, leg.

Being a pace of three time, the rhythm of the canter is different, and also certain muscles in the back and quarters have to work rather harder, so it is quite a good idea to do some cantering to make and develop these muscles. The working canter should be asked for on a large circle, not less than 15 metres (49 ft 3 ins) but this must all be done carefully to avoid overstrain and damage. Two, or three, turns at the canter and then back into trot, with plenty of free walk in between times. Remember, schooling exercises, like gymnastics, are quite hard work, and muscles should be worked to develop them, not simply tire them. A tired or sore horse, will soon start resisting.

When considering exercises for the older horse, the repertoire is almost endless. Even though if you are working in an older horse on the lunge, much of the work will be to loosen him up, so need not, in fact should not, be too collected. All the paces and their transitions can be practiced, working, medium and collected, plus lateral bending on the circle. The horse's balance can be improved, his head and neck carriage worked on, the engagement of his hind legs activated. The more supple the horse becomes, and the more he can engage his quarters, the smaller the circle he can work on, thus learning to collect himself. As he carries more weight on his quarters, so his neck should come up and the forehand become lighter. By increasing and decreasing the size of circles — working in a not too fast trot — decreasing down to a volte

8 metres (26 ft 3 ins) and out to 10 to 12 metres (32 ft 10 ins
to 39 ft 5 ins), this raising and lightening should be achieved.
Lateral bending is achieved by bringing the forehand in a
little and pushing the quarters away (shorten the rein and
hold the whip towards the ribs) thus causing the horse to
cross the inside hind leg in front of the outside hind leg. This
causes flexion of the quarter muscles, the back muscles and
also those covering the ribs. This exercise, like so many others,
should be carried out very carefully and not for too long — a
few steps at a time — then let the horse trot on and stretch
his neck right out and down, which he will almost certainly
want to do after the exertion of the exercise. Do not put the
horse into too acute an angle either. Nearly all this work can
be done without side reins, but they can be introduced once
the horse goes well in his working paces to improve his
balance. Some trainers introduce them earlier than others.

SIDE REINS, THEIR USE AND FITTING

The use of side reins can be a controversial subject, with advocates both for and against their use.

One thing is certain however. Side reins should not be misused. Correctly used, they certainly help to give results. Once it has been decided to use them, then they must be put on so that there is an even contact between the bit and the girth, or roller. If a horse has never had them on before, then they must be on the loose side until he is used to the feel of them. Never must they be attached in such a way as to pull a horse's head in. Even with a confirmed "star gazer", he should be encouraged to lower his head gradually. The whole idea of side reins is to put the horse "on the bit", by working him up to it by the engagement of the hind legs, that is from behind.

So, for the horse who is ready to have side reins on, attach them loosely and work him quietly for a few minutes gradually shortening the reins until the required contact is achieved which in turn will give the head carriage required. Obviously with a young horse one does not ask for too much shortening of the horse's base, whereas with a more advanced horse a considerably shorter base can be achieved. In this case the side reins must not be attached too low. Some lungeing rollers have rings on them at differing levels, for this very reason. In general I think it will be found that a good place to attach the reins is just above the girth buckles. This will prevent them slipping down. Unless one is specifically trying to work a horse's back and neck, I do not like to see side reins on too low, preferring the horse to keep as natural a head carriage as possible, yet improving and developing a good outline together with better balance and control.

PLATE 9

Close up of how the side reins are attached to the saddle for lungeing.

On a large circle the reins can be of almost equal length, but on a smaller circle the inside rein should be a little shorter, about 4 holes. However, the inside rein should never be too much shorter, because, if it is, all the horse's weight will be thrown onto the inside shoulder, his quarters will swing away and he will go on his forehand. One must observe vigilantly to see that this does not happen.

The trot, being a pace of two time, is the correct pace at which to use side reins, because it is the only pace at which the horse can move, and yet, keep his head still. Both at the walk, and at the canter, he moves his head from side to side just a little, so by rights if the reins are left on at either canter or walk they should be loosened so as not to cause unnecessary, and often damaging, pressure on the mouth.

If one is practising transitions from trot to walk, and vice versa, provided the side reins are not too tight and you make sure to push the hind legs well up, then the horse will learn through the lungeing work to give nicely to your hand at these transitions; which of course when done mounted are asked for from the leg aids, the hands only resisting after the leg aid has been applied. The same thing applies in lungeing, the whip replacing the leg.

One must be careful to observe that the horse does not come behind the bit and over-bend. If he does, either the reins are too short, the horse tired, or the trainer not keeping the horse's hind legs active.

HOW THE HORSE REACTS

Although this book is primarily about how to use the lungeing rein, I think it is worth digressing for a page or two on the subject of the way, or the reasons why, horses react.

It is reasonably easy to learn to handle a rein, but it is another matter to understand a horse's ways. Any successful trainer needs to be able to do both.

The horse, we are told, is the most willing of creatures. But he does need to understand our wishes. The horse's brain is small, and he has limited intelligence. As his reasoning powers are limited, and the horse is so quick to learn, it is important that we teach him the right things, as it is very hard, in fact nearly impossible mentally, for the horse to un-learn.

One can develop the horse's brain, and certainly gain his co-operation through gaining his confidence. This entails patience on the part of the trainer, and although one should always look for progress, try not to ask the horse to perform movements that he is incapable of, because he will almost certainly react by resisting. Never work in such a way as to fluster, or rush, a horse. He will react by panicking, and again, the result will not be good.

The horse has two very marked instincts. The fear of pain, and the homing (or herding) instinct. If, for instance, the horse thinks he is going to be hurt, maybe by the whip, or by some outside object, he will react in the only way he knows, by trying to run away. Therefore, the confidence required by the horse to accept objects of which he is frightened must be built up slowly and by degrees. Once acceptance is learnt by the horse he will, unless frightened in the meantime, retain that acceptance. The idea of rewarding the horse, by a pat, a word, or a titbit will help. Be quick to reward and slow to punish. Try and analyse problems. Ask yourself why the horse has done what he has. The reason will probably give you the answer to your problem. For instance, if a horse is throwing his head up and down, do not just hit him. Have a look at his mouth, and see if his teeth are hurting him, or whether the bit or the cavasson are pinching. The horse, in all probability, is reacting to pain. The source of the pain should be removed, which will then rectify the fault.

The horse has a number of senses which we should learn to understand, even a little. Hearing in the horse is very acute, often causing a horse to shy or jump at a noise, which we can hardly hear ourselves. Similarly, our tone of voice when giving commands will cause a reaction from the horse. A harsh, rough voice will result in a violent reaction.

The sense of sight in the horse, is something which I believe is not taken into account enough in horse training. A horse **is** very observant and long sighted — again, a development of his early days, when flight was his only means of avoiding danger.

We know that the horse sees to the side and behind him, unlike man, and when he looks to the front the focal point of synchronisation is some way in front of his head. A horse does not focus very close to his head, and often when you get very close to him with an object for him to inspect, he will smell it, as smell is for the horse another important sense.

So, if you want a horse to learn about something, a new jump for example, or even his saddle, let him smell it.

Some horses are undoubtedly more aware of sharp shadows and bright objects than others. Also one might believe that horses with broad foreheads focus differently to those with narrow foreheads. Remember that, as the horse can see behind him, the position the trainer takes, and the way he uses his whip are all observed, and acted upon by the horse.

The sense of feel which includes not only the feel of the

tack, or the whip, but the feel of vibrations is well marked in the horse. A touch of the whip, and a slight movement by the trainer may be enough indication to many horses, to move. In nature, the horse is looking all the time for self preservation. Hence, if he feels false ground under him, that indicates danger and he will not continue and will try to leave the area. If we want to make the horse accept our wishes then he has to some extent to overcome his natural fears – a strong horseman may be able to force a horse into subjection, but a patient one who understands the horse and gains his confidence will achieve a far better result.

The instincts and the senses all ought to be taken into account, and used to help us gain our result. Clarity and simplicity are what horses like and understand. Work on the lungeing rein is particularly good for establishing this understanding, as well as developing the mental and physical attributes of the horse.

Thoroughbred horses are by nature, hot blooded and have very quick reactions. Thus the margin of error in training a thoroughbred is very small indeed. But wonderful results can be achieved in many areas of equitation, working with thoroughbreds, on account of their quickness and ability. Many of the Continental breeds have been developed to include a large measure of docility – the German breeds are an example – and this has been done specifically to aid training, and usefulness as saddle and carriage horses, the thoroughbred being developed for racing, where speed and quick reactions are at a premium. No two horses are exactly the same in temperament, and no doubt much of the fascination of horses, and their training, lies in this fact.

VII

RELAXING AND DEVELOPING MUSCLES

Having written about the horse's mental reactions, it is I feel a good idea to now have a look at his physical make up.

When lungeing a horse, it is most important that certain muscles are being used and certain other ones do less. In the young horse the muscles should be stretched and made as long as possible so that they can be fully developed. It is the stretching and contracting, alternately, of a muscle which develops it.

The muscles which come to mind as the easiest ones to recognize, and also the most important to develop correctly, are the crest muscle of the neck and the lumbar muscles of the back. On the lunge the horse should go forwards evenly, with the hind feet tracking up to the fore feet. The criteria of a relaxed horse which is using the neck and back muscles correctly are: that the horse is, if wearing a bit, accepting the bit quietly and with some white froth showing at his lips; the mouth is of course, closed; the ears are in a relaxed position; and the tail is carried away from the quarters — not tucked down, in which case the back is set and rigid — and just swinging from side to side with the movement of the horse. If these criteria are shown, the horse is, so to speak, at our disposal mentally and physically.

Horses vary as to how long they need to be worked before achieving these criteria. Some take 10 minutes, others up to 20, or even 30 minutes. The lumbar muscles along the back should appear soft and springy, not hard and rigid. Many horses suffer from hard backs, and many older ones, who, when young, never learned to relax their back muscles, find it difficult to achieve this softness later. Learn to look at a horse's back, it will tell you a great deal. The tension all along

PLATE 10

The more collected position asked for in the advanced horse.
Note the rounded top outline, and the engagement of the left
hind leg.

the spine should be even, each vertebrae fitting into the next one without undue pressure. It is not out of place to say here, how very delicate the mechanism of a horse's back is and how much damage can be caused by wrong or rough use of it. This cannot be stressed enough.

Another area to look at, and which will show you if your horse is relaxing properly, are the stomach muscles. These should not be held tightly, as if the horse was holding his breath. It is very interesting to notice the difference in the muscles after a few minutes of work. The nice even looking trot, as described earlier, is the pace at which to achieve these results.

The hindquarters of the horse are very important to work on, and a well schooled horse will, or should, develop tremendous second thighs. Also, the area above the tail, on either side of the back bone should become well rounded. By decreasing and enlarging the lungeing circles, and increasing and decreasing the length of the strides (working to medium trot) these muscles can all be developed.

In the lengthened strides, the hind leg and the muscles of the quarters should have been developed so as to stretch out behind at the moment of the fullest length of the stride. The hocks must of course be able to engage well under the horse at the other extreme (diagonal) of the lengthened stride, whilst the shoulder muscles should be developed enough to stretch forwards. But before this can be properly achieved the back and neck muscles should be working correctly. That may take some weeks, or even months to achieve, but it is so often the level of acceptability, plus the time available, that determines how long we can take with our training programme.

VIII

CAVALETTI

Trotting poles and cavaletti are an important aid in the schooling of a horse for whatever purpose.

In the last two chapters, I have discussed the mental and physical make up of the horse and how important the back muscles in particular are, and of the need to develop and work all muscles correctly.

Undoubtedly, poles set on the ground are most helpful and can be used with great success by a horse being lunged.

I will not go back over the requirements needed, before a horse is considered ready to work over cavaletti, except to say the horse should be well used to going quietly on the lunge. In the early stages of training, I would require the horse to work without side reins for cavaletti work. I would look for a long neck, good engagement of the hind legs, and above all, an even stride. The multiple cavaletti are in fact a mechanical means of putting the horse into a certain length of stride, that is long or short, and a criteria of this development is that he does not alter the length of his stride, either approaching, over, or coming away from the poles. This naturally takes time to obtain, and the distance between the cavaletti must be correctly spaced. At the same time the horse should, by virtue of the fact that he has to raise his hind legs and his fore legs as he passes over the poles, give with the lumbar muscles along the back, hence the importance of cavaletti work for this development.

To start with I would introduce the horse to just one pole, and that lying flat on the ground, about 15 to 20 centimetres (6 to 8 ins), not in the higher position of 30 centimetres (1 ft) to which a proper cavaletti with X sides can be placed. Once the horse will walk quietly over one pole, I would introduce another about 1·22 metres (4 ft) beyond it. It is most important to watch the horse's length of stride. Some have much longer, or shorter, strides than others. Then the poles must be altered accordingly. Once the horse will walk quietly over the two poles, these can be spaced at about 1·47 metres (4 ft 10 ins) apart for trotting. The same quiet rhythm is required for trotting. If the horse is inclined to rush at the poles only let him go over them every second or third time round on the circle, looking in between times for the return to relaxation. If, on the other hand, the horse is sluggish, look to see if he is tracking up correctly and see that he is, then he will probably cross the poles correctly, and it will be noticed, begin to take up a correct attitude, carrying his head and neck in a nice position of his own accord. Once you see the horse beginning to do that, then you are achieving something.

As the horse progresses then you can build up your line of cavaletti to four. This number I find usually gives the result required, five or six being rather too many to deal with on the lunge.

If you are working in the riding school, it may be easiest to put your poles alongside the long wall and straighten the horse out to trot down the line. This is the easiest approach. If you are working on a circle then you must graduate your poles to form part of the circle. At a later stage of training, when the horse is wearing side reins for work on the flat, he can also work in them over the cavaletti. This will help him to use certain muscles in the back and neck. It is very important to watch that the horse does not try to hollow his back and come either above or below the bit in this type of exercise; that is, by either raising his head too high or putting his head into his chest, with his hocks away out behind him. This is a considerable danger if the side reins are too tightly adjusted.

All horse training needs concentration and lungeing is no

exception. It is by observing things that you can put them right.

There are varieties of layout for cavaletti, the simplest of which are described here.

For walking over, a line of 1, 2, 3 or 4 cavaletti laid flat at 1·14 to 1·22 metres (3 ft 9 ins to 4 ft) apart.

For trotting over, a line of 1, 2, 3 or 4 calvaletti laid flat at 1·4 to 1·47 metres (4 ft 6 ins to 4 ft 10 ins) approximately, apart.

Cavaletti can be spaced much closer for collected work, at the trot, to 0·8 to 1 metre (2 ft 8 ins to 3 ft 3 ins) approximately, but I would not recommend these extreme distances until the horse is in an advanced state of training, at very least until he is in his second year of schooling.

The same applies to spreading out the distances to around 1·52 metres (5 ft) or more for extended paces. Although, here again, to improve a horse's paces the cavaletti can be spaced out, or in, a little to encourage lengthening or shortening, but not in such extreme degree as to cause the horse to trip, or put in a short stride within the set of cavaletti.

If the cavaletti are turned up to 25 or 30 centimetres (10 or 12 ins) in height, then they are much more difficult for the horse to negotiate. The horse should not attempt to jump, the purpose being to improve the paces. For ordinary purposes, a more suitable height is 10 or 15 centimetres (4 or 6 ins).

Some people advocate cavaletti placed at odd, or different, distances. My own view is, that if you put them at different distances, then make these distances possible ones for the horse to negotiate. An event horse certainly must learn to be both agile and clever. An exercise I would prefer is to take the third pole of a set of four away, thus leaving the horse with a stride which is not organized by the cavaletti, thus the horse must organize his stride himself. Also, occasionally, shorten up the distance 3 to 5 centimetres (1 to 2 ins approximately), so as to develop a true ability to shorten, rather than by tripping a horse up.

There are other ways of dealing with the problems of cleverness and agility, which are outside the use of cavaletti.

The horse should, on arriving at a cavaletti, "take off", so to speak, an even distance from it, and the middle of his body should be over the cavaletti as the hind and fore feet of a particular diagonal are on the ground. He should not hit the pole with either his front or hind foot coming too close. With an even stride and with the horse developing his own eye to some extent, then the trainer can help by concentrating to see that the approach stride is correct. Then the cavaletti work can be very useful indeed. However, if the horse is allowed to rush about, and to trip over cavaletti with no plan in the layout, then the work can be positively harmful.

As well as balancing and suppling the horse, cavaletti are also an excellent progression towards first jumping lessons. Cavaletti lessons, varying from between 15 and 40 minutes each, can be practised two to three times a week, as a variation from the ordinary routine of lunge work, the difficulty of the lesson graded in accordance with the stage of training of the horse involved.

IX

FAULTS AND PROBLEMS

Having discussed various methods of fitting tack and ways of schooling horses correctly, I feel it is important now to discuss some aspects of re-schooling, because it is so often the horse which has a fault, or is resisting, that one is trying to help.

The most important things, in my opinion, are firstly, to be able to know how to lunge and to recognize when a horse is going correctly; and secondly, to have some idea of the conformation of a horse. It goes without saying that one's own temper must always be under control and one's actions, quiet yet quick. These are all things which can be improved with practice, and a furtherance of knowledge. Someone who is a novice should be able to become reasonably good at lungeing — it may be necessary to take some expert advice — but ordinary lungeing is not beyond the scope of the every day rider. The more specialised lungeing, like all specialised work, needs more study and practice.

Faults and resistances can be caused by pain, and the physical inability to carry out a movement. Forcing horses into unnatural positions, in themselves will cause bad habits to develop.

There are two good guides, as to whether a horse is going correctly. First, if his footfalls are even; and second, if his "outline" is rounded. That is, the crest muscles of the neck should be arched, yet the head be in a natural and not over-bent position. The lumbar muscles should be soft and "rippling", with the hind feet stepping well up to the mark of the front hooves. To correct any fault, I feel it is important to have his picture in your mind's eye, and always work towards it.

A horse which over-bends will often stop doing so if he is

allowed to stretch his neck and carry his own head. But to improve the whole horse, it will be necessary to see that his hind legs are active, for when you go to ride him, or even lunge him with side reins to become "on the bit", it is from the activity of the hind legs that the impulsion should come. A word of warning should be sounded here however. There are two ends to a horse, front and rear. It is the equality, or evenness, of stride of the hind and the front legs which is wanted. Not an over abundance of hind leg activity, and a horse all unbalanced in front — a fault which is seen but not always readily recognized. Then there is the horse with a beautiful carriage in front, and no activity behind. The latter is easier to spot, because the hind feet do not track up to the hoof prints of the front feet. In the former, the front end locks itself and the horse over-bends, or goes very heavy in the bit. Neither is really desirable. So do try and watch and see how even the strides are of all the horse's legs.

A horse which is hollow backed, will also probably not track up, and will carry his head too high. A loose pair of side reins may help here, as also will work over cavaletti, which will encourage the horse to look down and to loosen his back muscles.

A word here on the conformation of the horse. Two things come immediately to mind. Short backed horses are invariably difficult to make entirely supple, because their muscles are very strong and hard. Long backed horses, although very comfortable to ride, are often weak in their backs, and rather difficult to balance. Additionally, they are often very long striding, and in the thoroughbred, a long stride is often very impulsive, and hence needs tact when handling. Thin long muscles are weaker than thick short ones. The conformation of the horse's jaws and throat often give rise to problems. A fairly wide throat, and strong, wide apart jaw bones is a definite attribute, because there is room for the horse to flex correctly at the poll. When he does so there is pressure on the salivary glands, which press on the big rounded jaw bones under the throat. These bones sometimes have quite rough edges. You can feel this for yourself, if you run your fingers along them. If the jaws are naturally narrow, it will follow that there is probably not room for him to comfortably close his mouth, without biting it. Consequently, this often means mouth problems, especially if the drop noseband is too tight. Teeth of course, should be regularly attended to.

These are just one or two points of conformation which may have a bearing on how your horse goes, or rather, why he reacts the way he does.

A useful exercise to develop lateral suppleness in the horse's back, is the turn-on-the-forehand on the lunge, already described in Chapter IV.

There are many other exercises, such as making the circle smaller and larger, most of which were also discussed in Chapter IV.

My advice regarding faults is, that if you wish to try and correct them, via the lunge line, first put the horse onto a fairly large circle 15 to 20 metres (50 to 66 ft) in walk and later in trot. Encourage him to stretch his neck, muscles and back in particular. This is putting the horse into a natural position, and one which is easy for him. Once he learns relaxation and self balance for a few minutes each day like this, then one can ask for a more balanced, or more collected, position when the horse is "on the bit", that is, on a shorter base.

This can only be achieved in the long run by eliminating all resistances and making it easy for the horse in the first place. There may be short cuts, but I do not believe these really last, and in the long term, are often detrimental. A little patience and ground work will help enormously. One usually works the horse to begin with, without side reins, or with them just loosely adjusted. Later on with the shorter base, the side reins do have a job to do, but not by pulling the horse's head in. In fact, even with the spoiled or difficult horse, I would put him back to "square one" and do the elementary exercises, which are described in Chapter II.

There are often things which happen when lungeing, that I would term, problems. There may be the time when the horse turns in and faces you. If you have a helper, they can lead the horse on, but the problem could have occurred because you were not in the proper position to keep the horse moving forwards, that is, not in line with the horse's inside hip. The signal to slow down, as was mentioned earlier, is to move into line with the horse's shoulder. Sometimes a horse will turn in very quickly, so one needs to be alert and watching what one is doing to prevent this happening. Sometimes a touch, or the sight of the whip near the hocks will teach the horse to move on. But in any case be prepared to move within a prescribed area — and sometimes well outside it!

When I have a difficult horse to lunge, I try to take him into the corner of the school and work him in walk on a small circle with the walls to help keep him in position. Sometimes one literally has to walk the horse in front of one, but it is very interesting how soon such a horse will give in and do what you want — once he understands and when treated quietly and not flustered.

On a very small circle, and as the horse moves off, a horse can, if he so wishes, kick out and this can be dangerous. My advice in such a case, is to be careful with a horse you do not know, and in any case try to instill into all horses you work with, the desirability of moving off quietly. If you have a fresh young horse who wants to have a "fling" keep him out on a big enough circle, and keep him going until he has finished his antics. With a strong horse being lunged whilst still fresh and in an open space it may be wise to attach the lunge rein to the bit rings in some way, and additionally to have an extra long and strong rein. Personally with a horse such as this, I would always lunge him in an enclosed space. Once a horse learns to get away, it is not only dangerous, but he will certainly try to do so again.

There are obvious advantages to lungeing on a dirt floor, such as sand or peat. One advantage is that the horse will not stop and try to eat it, as he might well do on grass. Another is that the actual footing may well be better. Grass for instance can be very nice, but it can be slippery also.

X

JUMPING

An extremely good way of teaching a horse to jump is to start him doing so on the lunge.

Obviously the horse should first of all be taught to lunge on a circle, to be reasonably familiar with what is wanted and to be obedient to his trainer.

Two things need a little thought. First, the building and siting of fences; second, and more importantly, the trainer should have some knowledge of how a horse should jump, and have a clear picture in his mind's eye of the correct style for the jump, of the bascule, the fold of the legs and the calm, balanced approach.

A young horse should learn to like jumping and to use himself to the best advantage physically. He should use his back, tuck up his legs and stretch his neck. He should approach the fence calmly. So, much of the work on the lunge for jumping should be done from a trot, to give the horse time to see the jump, and to allow him to balance himself. Later on, when mounted, the horse should approach the fence and use himself with confidence and calmness.

A horse can jump a height of about 1·40 metres (4ft 6ins) from a trot.

An older horse can be reschooled on the lunge, over a fence, to restore both confidence and calmness.

When a horse jumps in the correct style, he should perform a parabola, a half circle through the air, from take off point to landing point. This parabola is best peformed when the horse uses his head, neck and back in what is described as a bascule. So, where does one start to try and achieve this?

The answer, in my opinion, is to be found by walking the horse over a pole laid on the ground. This pole should be put in such a place as to encourage the horse to go over it. That place is usually just after the corner of the manège or school. Have two uprights, the left hand (or inner) one with a pole balanced on it, first to act as a wing and second, to allow the lunge line to smoothly pass over the upright. *(See Figure 1).* The right, or outer, upright should be close to the wall, the wall therefore acting as an extra aid to keep the horse straight. The horse will commence by working on the left rein as it is the easiest, and the corner will again, be an aid to the approach — the pole being some 4·57 metres (15 ft) or so beyond the corner on the "long" side. Later, as the fence becomes higher, put the poles further away from the corner. Also the horse should be worked on the right rein, as well as the left.

As one progresses beyond the pole on the ground stage, a little cross pole, with a ground line becomes suitable. Some people prefer to put a pole some 2·74, 5·48, or 6·40 metres (9, 18 or 21 ft) in front of this little jump. My own preference however is to wait a little for this "help". For a tiny little fence of between 30 and 45 centimetres (12 and 18 ins), the young horse should learn to negotiate it by using his own brain, although I sometimes do use a pole for bigger fences.

The advantage of lungeing a horse, is to help develop the horse's own initiative, without the rider. Later, when ridden, a ground rail some distance away can be of very distinct value, and is also useful under certain circumstances in correcting faults.

Faults may include: not looking down at the fence on the approach; or a difficult length of natural stride (too long or too short); or one may be trying to gain the confidence of a horse that puts in a short stride when he could easily stand off.

Once the horse will pop over the little cross poles happily, the real test of developing his ability is the parallel bars. To

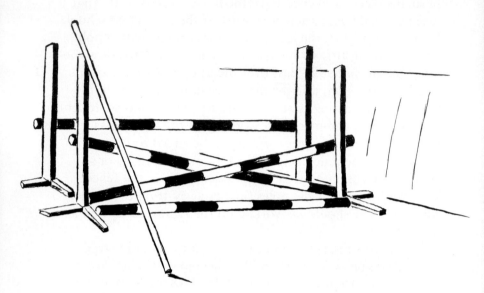

FIGURE 1

Suitable jump for lungeing a reasonably advanced young jumper. A rail has been set behind the cross-bars to give extra height and width. Note the pole at left, positioned to allow the rein to pass over the uprights as the horse jumps the fence, and the side of the manège, right, is also used as a wing to prevent the horse running out.

begin with, I like them low, with the back rail just a shade higher than the front. Each time the horse jumps successfully, make the fence wider, just a centimetre or so at a time. Never over face the young horse. Stop when he has made a good jump. Reward your horse, when he has done well. These are the unwritten laws of horse training.

The height of the fence will depend to a large extent on the horse's ability, temperament and degree of training.

For a very young horse, a 3 or 4 year old, 60 centimetres (2 ft) high and up to 1·52 metres (5 ft) wide is big enough. But only commence the lesson with a much smaller fence, say, 45 centimetres (18 ins) high and 60 centimetres (2 ft) wide.

For a more advanced horse, a 4 to 5 year old, the fence could go to between 91 and 122 centimetres (3 to 4 ft approximately) high, and about 1·83 metres (6 ft) wide. The latter is a big enough fence for a training exercise, especially when working in trot. Putting a bar diagonally across the parallels to encourage the horse to jump over, not into, the fence is a useful aid.

A horse should not jump on every circle, to attempt it will only make him rush. Work the horse calmly, let him trot quietly up to the fence, pop over, then go calmly round again for a few more circuits, gradually working back to a good approach position and repeat the exercise. If you have a helper to alter the fence, so much the better. It is an awful nuisance to have to stop the horse and alter a fence, but it can be done if necessary. When doing so, always check that the cups, or blocks, for the poles are in such a position that they do not fix the poles against the uprights. This could be very dangerous.

Lungeing the young horse two or three times a week will not only teach him how to jump, but will also build up the proper muscles for jumping.

It is important to have a long enough lunge line, because it is bad to have to run to keep up with a horse which gives a buck on landing, and worse to let him go. The lunge line should be attached to the cavasson, not to the bit.

As well as the classic parallel bars, it is easy to introduce the young horse to all sorts of fences, gates, walls and so on. In trying to determine what is the logical progression in the training of a jumper, I think one can sum it up thus: first, confidence; second, development and use of the long and very strong back muscles; third, teaching the horse to elevate in front; fourth, introducing the horse to strange fences.

All this can be achieved, via the lunge, without the weight of the rider to interfere with the horse. A very important advantage.

XI

OTHER WAYS OF ATTACHING THE REIN

As has already been discussed, schooling a horse from the ground, is really a convenient way of trying to counteract difficulties.

Probably, of all the work from the ground, lungeing is the most easily used.

The work-in-hand, as described by the great French scholar, General Decarpentry, in his book *Academic Equitation*, could be said to be the most effective method when in the right hands.

Alternatively, the work on long reins as used by the Danish teacher and judge Mr. Schmit Jensen, and by myself, (see *The Art of Long Reining*) is also a very rewarding way of schooling, but it is difficult for people to learn.

Ground work such as work in the pillars, is not well understood, except in Vienna, and by one or two connoisseurs, and for present day competitive work can best be described as an anachronism. Most of us are not aspiring to produce the highest classical airs.

So, having discussed objectives in previous chapters, I will now conclude by describing one or two different ways of adjusting the lungeing rein. Always remembering that by adjusting the rein in these various ways, one is at once concentrating on the front end of the horse; and the danger lies in over concentration there; that is, one can start "pulling in the head" as opposed to pushing up the hind legs and an acceptance of the bit.

It is fair to say that the methods of lungeing described earlier in this book are those advocated in both Germany and Scandinavia. What the following description owes its origins to, is the French system which places such importance on the

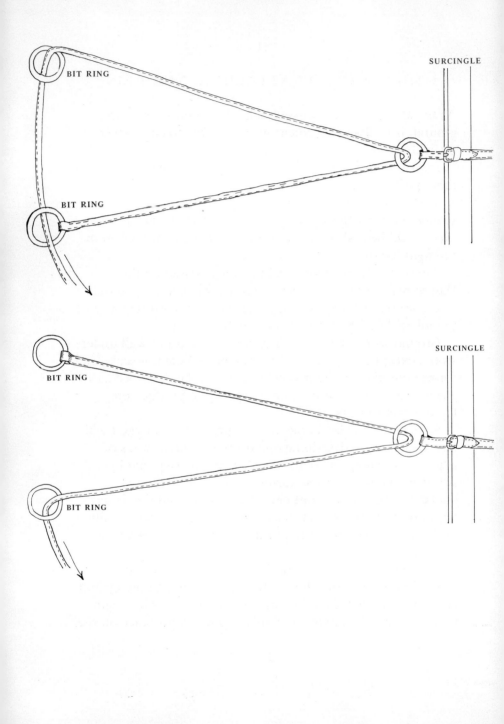

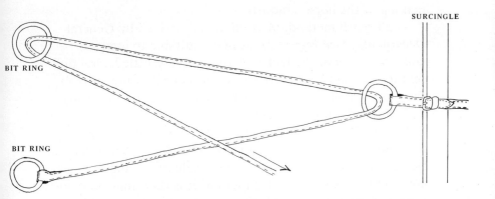

FIGURE 2 *(opposite, top)*

General Decarpentry's Method 1, of attaching the reins (on the left rein), he describes as being suitable to increase collection. This is due to the fact that there is very little lateral pull on the rein, because there is a good deal of pressure on the outside rein. Thus, the horse must use himself truly and go straight up to the bit.

FIGURE 3 *(opposite, bottom)*

Decarpentry's Method 2, again on the left rein, is useful and fairly easily managed, to induce a better lateral flexion from the horse. This is due to the inside rein being of considerable bearing. In this method, it is very important to notice whether the horse's quarters are swinging outside the track of the circle, and whether the lateral flexion being asked for is too severe, i.e. the neck bending too much.

FIGURE 4 *(above)*

Decarpentry's Method 3, on the left rein, is for a well schooled horse, who is supple and can flex easily. It is used to prevent over flexion, by a bearing being kept on the outside rein. This is quite a difficult arrangement to manage. If things do go wrong, a rather violent backward tension can occur.

making of the horse's mouth.

The French method, Method 1, is described by General Decarpentry *(see Figure 2)*, as being suitable to increase collection, due to the fact that there is very little lateral pull on the rein, and because there is a good deal of pressure on the outside rein, and thus, the horse must use himself truly and go straight up to the bit.

Method 2 *(see Figure 3)*, again from General Decarpentry, is useful, and fairly easily managed, to induce a better lateral flexion from the horse, due to the inside rein being of considerable bearing. In this method it is very important to notice whether the horse's quarters are swinging out, and whether the flexion being asked is too severe.

Method 3 *(see Figure 4)*, is for a well schooled horse, who is supple and can flex easily, and used to prevent over flexion, by a bearing being kept on the outside rein. Quite difficult to manage as, if the horse starts to over-flex, or things go wrong, a rather violent backward tension can occur.

All these foregoing methods are subject to the horse wearing a surcingle with a ring attachment at the withers.

In Method 1, General Decarpentry tells us he worked his horse for 5 minutes on each rein, rested the horse on a slack rein and completed the lesson by working 2 to 3 minutes more on each rein. First, putting the horse onto the bit, and making what he calls "a few slight oppositions to the hand when the pace is lengthened", that is, if the horse ran or quickened and thus was incorrectly lengthening. Finally, with the horse on the bit, allowing some correctly cadenced lengthened paces, the hand giving, but not losing, contact.

The second arrangement was used particularly for increase and decrease of circles, whilst the third arrangement, together with the second, was for straightening the horse, and improving the already schooled horse. General Decarpentry advocates working the horse 2 to 3 minutes on the concave side, and 7 to 8 minutes on the convex side.

So, it will be seen that this "French" system of arranging the rein was not haphazard. There was an end in view. It is, I think, a fairly difficult method, but must be included in any book purporting to describe lungeing as a whole.

CONCLUSION

I have tried to make this book clear and concise, so that those who read it feel they can go out and try the things I have described. One has to cover, or at least try to cover, all aspects and standards. For me, working horses from the ground, whether on long reins or on the lunge line, gives a particular satisfaction. In long reins one can achieve a very high degree of training — higher than in lungeing, but lungeing has a very great deal to recommend it. It is used in most Continental countries for much basic ground work and that is where its value really lies.

ABOUT THE AUTHOR

Sylvia Stanier began riding at an early age, and grew up with a hunting and showing background. Sam Marsh was one of her first teachers, and she has based much of her work on the principles of Lt.-Col. "Joe" Dudgeon.

Miss Stanier has travelled widely in both Europe and North and Central America. She has trained with Schmit-Jensen and Oliveira, and attended the Olympic Games equestrian events in Japan in 1964 and in Mexico in 1968.

In 1965, she won the Ladies Championship at the Dublin Show on Bachelor Gay. Riding Lough Thorn in 1966, she won the Lightweight Hunter Championship in Dublin, and later the same year, at Wembley, she gave a Long Reining Display with Le Marquis, during the Horse of the Year Show. In 1967 she won the Dressage Championship of Ireland, on Fanny.

For many years Miss Stanier worked at the Burton Hall Establishment. She has written a number of articles and books on training and riding, including the companion volume to this book, *The Art of Long Reining*.

Sylvia Stanier lives at Market Harborough in Leicestershire, where she conducts training and riding courses for both novice and advanced pupils.

Readers of this book who wish to be informed about new and forthcoming publications on horses and horsemanship are invited to send their names and addresses to:

J. A. ALLEN & CO. LTD.,
1, Lower Grosvenor Place,
Buckingham Palace Road,
London, SW1W 0EL.